Effective Communication at Work

15 Essential Email Templates for
Business Communication

EMMA TAYLOR

DISCLAIMER

The contents of the book "**Effective Communication at Work: 15 Essential Email Templates for Business Communication,**" including, but not limited to, the text, graphics, images, and other material contained within, are the exclusive property of the author and are protected under international copyright laws.

TABLE OF CONTENTS

INTRODUCTION

In the digital age, where information travels at the speed of light and connections are made with the click of a button, effective communication stands as a linchpin in achieving professional success. At the heart of this communication landscape lies a humble yet potent tool—**email**. Whether you're a budding entrepreneur forging partnerships or a seasoned corporate professional navigating intricate deals, the skill of crafting impactful business emails is a cornerstone of your journey.

Welcome to **"Effective Communication at Work: 15 Essential Email Templates for Business Communication."** This book is your gateway to unraveling the complexities of crafting business emails that leave a lasting impression, foster connections, and catalyze actions. These templates aren't mere words on a screen; they're bridges that link you to your goals, your audience, and your aspirations.

Within these pages, you'll embark on a journey through the complex world of email business writing. We will traverse diverse scenarios, industries, and interactions, ensuring that every template aligns with your ambitions. Whether you're initiating a conversation, nurturing relationships, addressing inquiries, or advocating your ideas, you'll find templates tailored to your specific needs.

While these templates serve as the foundations, remember that they're designed to be molded by your creativity and authenticity. We provide templates and a compass that directs you toward crafting emails that reflect your personality, resonate with your recipients, and achieve your objectives.

As we embark on this journey together, remember that every email you send carries the potential to shape relationships, forge alliances, and propel your aspirations forward. The realm of business email writing is a canvas awaiting your unique brushstrokes.

Are you ready to unlock the art of email business writing? Let's delve right into it and uncover the threads that weave communication mastery into the fabric of your success.

1. PROFESSIONAL INTRODUCTION

In the realm of business, first impressions carry substantial weight. Your initial contact with a potential client, partner, or colleague sets the tone for your relationship moving forward. Crafting a professional introduction email that resonates requires careful consideration of both content and tone.

A well-crafted professional introduction conveys your identity and purpose and demonstrates your professionalism and respect for the recipient's time. Whether you're reaching out for a potential collaboration, networking opportunity, or simply initiating a connection, a thoughtful introduction can pave the way for meaningful interactions.

Guidelines for Crafting an Effective Professional Introduction

- **Start with a Strong Subject Line**: Your subject line should be concise and engaging, capturing the recipient's interest. Consider mentioning a shared interest or benefit in the subject to encourage them to open the email.

- **Personalize Your Greeting**: Address the recipient by name and tailor your greeting to the appropriate formality for your relationship.

- **Offer Context and Connection**: Briefly explain who you are, your role, and the purpose of your email. If you have a mutual connection or shared interest, mention it to establish rapport.

- **Highlight Mutual Benefits**: Clearly articulate how the recipient could benefit from connecting with you. Highlight the value you can bring to the table and how your interaction can be a win-win situation.

- **Show Respect for Their Time**: Keep your introduction concise and to the point. Avoid overwhelming the recipient with excessive details.

- **Express Enthusiasm**: Convey your genuine interest in connecting and collaborating. Enthusiasm can be contagious and make your email more memorable.

- **Include a Call to Action (CTA)**: Provide a clear next step or action you'd like the recipient to take. This could be setting up a meeting, exploring a partnership, or requesting a brief phone call.

Template

Exploring Potential Collaboration in [Industry/Field]

Dear [Recipient's Name],

I hope this email finds you well. My name is [Your Name], and I am a [Your Position] at [Your Company]. I was impressed by your recent achievements in [Shared Interest or Industry] and wanted to explore potential collaboration opportunities.

As someone deeply invested in [Industry/Field], I believe that our expertise and perspectives could complement each other effectively. Your work in [Specific Achievement or Project] caught my attention, and I'm eager to discuss how we could combine our strengths with [Mutual Benefit or Goal].

If you're open to it, I'd love to schedule a brief call to explore our potential synergies further and exchange insights. Please let me know a convenient time for you, and I'll accommodate your schedule.

Thank you for considering this opportunity, and I look forward to working together. Should you have any questions or would like to connect, please feel free to reach out at [Your Email Address] or [Your Phone Number].

Best regards,

[Your Full Name]

[Your Position]

[Your Company]

[Your Contact Information]

2. INQUIRY AND INFORMATION REQUEST

In business, curiosity often sparks innovation, collaboration, and growth. Whether you're seeking to gather crucial data, explore potential partnerships, or expand your knowledge, crafting a well-structured inquiry and information request can open doors to valuable insights and opportunities.

A well-crafted inquiry goes beyond simply asking questions. It involves framing your curiosity in a way that shows genuine interest, respect for the recipient's expertise, and an understanding of the value they can provide. The goal is to spark a meaningful conversation or exchange of information that benefits both parties involved.

Key Components of an Effective Inquiry and Information Request:

- **Introduction:** Begin with a courteous and concise introduction that sets the tone for the email. State who you are and your connection, if any, to the recipient.

- **Clarity and Specificity:** Clearly outline the purpose of your inquiry. Be specific about the information you seek and why it's relevant to your goals or projects.

- **Value Proposition:** Explain why the recipient's expertise or information is valuable to you. Highlight the potential benefits of their input.

- **Context:** Provide context to help the recipient understand the background and importance of your inquiry. This helps them tailor their response more effectively.

- **Convenience:** Make it easy for the recipient to respond by suggesting a preferred mode of communication and offering flexibility in terms of timing.

- **Gratitude:** Express appreciation for their time and willingness to assist. A genuine show of gratitude can leave a positive impression.

Template

Seeking Expert Insight on [Specific Topic]

Dear [Recipient's Name],

I hope this email finds you well. My name is [Your Name], and I am a [Your Title/Role] at [Your Company Name]. I came across your work on [Specific Topic] and was truly impressed by your insights into [Specific Area of Expertise]. Your expertise in this field has inspired me to reach out.

I am currently [Brief Explanation of Your Project or Goal], and I believe your unique perspective could greatly enrich my understanding of [Specific Aspect]. I would be honored to learn from your experiences and insights.

If your schedule permits, I would love to schedule a brief call or exchange emails to discuss [Specific Questions or Topics]. I understand that your time is valuable, so please let me know what mode of communication works best for you and any preferred time slots.

As I move forward with [Your Project or Goal], your insights would be immensely valuable. Thank you in advance for considering my request. I genuinely appreciate your willingness to share your expertise.

Looking forward to the possibility of connecting and learning from you.

Warm regards,

[Your Name]

[Your Contact Information]

3. THANK YOU AND APPRECIATION EMAILS

In business communication, expressing gratitude and appreciation holds remarkable power. Beyond being polite gestures, thank you and appreciation emails serve as more than just tokens of good manners; they are strategic tools that can strengthen relationships, leave positive impressions, and foster ongoing collaboration.

In a world where digital interactions often dominate, sending a heartfelt thank you or acknowledgment can create a lasting impact. Whether you're expressing gratitude to a client for their trust, showing appreciation to a colleague for their assistance, or acknowledging the efforts of a partner, these emails humanize your interactions and contribute to building a culture of respect and goodwill.

Beyond the immediate benefits, such emails also lay the groundwork for future interactions. They create a positive memory that can be recalled in subsequent discussions, making it more likely that your recipients will respond positively to future requests or propositions. Remember, gratitude is a universal language that transcends industry and position. By incorporating thank you and appreciation emails into your communication repertoire, you position yourself as someone who values the contributions of others.

| Template

Appreciating the Opportunity to Collaborate

Dear [Client's Name],

I hope this email finds you well. I wanted to take a moment to express my sincere gratitude for choosing [Your Company Name] as your partner for [specific project or service]. We are truly excited about the prospect of working together and are committed to delivering results that exceed your expectations.

Your decision to entrust us with this endeavor means a great deal to us, and we are eager to demonstrate the value we can bring to your business. Our team is dedicated to ensuring the success of this project and achieving the goals we've set forth.

If there's anything specific you'd like to discuss or any questions you have as we move forward, please don't hesitate to contact me directly. I'm here to ensure seamless collaboration and address any concerns.

Once again, thank you for placing your trust in us. We look forward to a productive and successful partnership.

Warm regards,

[Your Name]

[Your Title]

[Your Contact Information]

4. COLD OUTREACH AND NETWORKING

Relationships are often the bedrock upon which success is built. Whether you're an entrepreneur seeking potential clients or a corporate professional aiming to expand your network, cold outreach and networking can be transformative. Let's explore the pivotal role of reaching out to new connections and nurturing relationships through strategic networking.

Unlocking Opportunities Through Cold Outreach

Cold outreach is about making initial contact with individuals or entities you have not previously interacted with. It's an avenue for introducing yourself, your business, or your offerings in a way that captures interest and opens the door to further communication. Cold outreach is an art that demands attention to detail, personalization, and the ability to convey value succinctly.

Strategic Networking: Building Bridges and Trust

Networking is more than just collecting business cards at events—it's about creating genuine connections that can potentially lead to collaborations, partnerships, or opportunities. Effective networking involves:

- Active listening.
- Understanding the needs of others.
- Finding ways to offer value before seeking it in return.

It's about nurturing relationships over time, building trust, and cultivating a network of resources that can enhance your professional journey.

Template

Exploring Potential Synergies for [Common Interest]

Dear [Recipient's Name],

I hope this email finds you well. My name is [Your Name], and I recently came across [mention something specific about the recipient's work or achievements that caught your attention].

I was truly impressed by your expertise in [mention the area of expertise]. Given your background, I believe there could be some exciting opportunities for collaboration between [Your Company/Project] and [Recipient's Company/Project]. Our combined strengths could potentially [mention a specific benefit, such as reaching a wider audience, innovating in a certain field, etc.].

I'd love to explore this further and discuss how our respective strengths could complement each other. Would you be available for a brief virtual meeting next week? Your insights would be invaluable in shaping the potential direction of this collaboration.

Looking forward to the possibility of working together. Please let me know your availability, and I'll coordinate the details accordingly.

Best regards,

[Your Name]

[Your Contact Information]

5. FOLLOW-UP FOR RELATIONSHIP BUILDING

E very interaction, every exchange of words, holds the potential to nurture a connection that can prove invaluable in the long run in the business world. And in email business writing, the follow-up email emerges as a powerful tool for strengthening these relationships.

Nurturing Connection Through Persistence

Imagine you've just met a potential client at a networking event. Your initial conversation was engaging and promising, but how do you ensure this connection doesn't fade into the background noise of business interactions? This is where the art of follow-up comes into play.

Following up after an initial interaction demonstrates your genuine interest and commitment. It shows that you value your connection and will invest the time and effort to continue the conversation. Whether it's a thank-you email, a reminder of a discussion point, or a suggestion for future collaboration, a well-crafted follow-up email can make a lasting impression.

Turning Prospects into Partners

In the world of sales, a single touchpoint is rarely enough to seal the deal. Potential clients may need time to consider their options, discuss them internally, or simply build trust with you. This is where a series of well-timed and considerate follow-up emails can make a significant difference.

You can position yourself as a resource and build credibility by offering additional value in each follow-up. Perhaps you share a relevant article, offer insights into their industry, or provide a solution to a challenge they mentioned. Each follow-up demonstrates your dedication to their success and reaffirms your expertise.

The Balance of Persistence and Respect

Of course, there's a fine line between persistent and pushy. The goal is to maintain a level of frequency that keeps you in their minds without overwhelming them. It is key to crafting a follow-up that balances being informative, engaging, and respectful of their time.

With the right approach, follow-up emails can transform prospects into partners, turn casual acquaintances into valuable connections, and elevate your business relationships. So, as you navigate the world of email business writing, remember the significance of the follow-up—your bridge to building lasting and fruitful relationships.

Template

Continuing Our Conversation: [Topic of Discussion]

Dear [Recipient's Name],

I hope this email finds you well. It was truly a pleasure connecting with you at [Event/Location] and discussing [Briefly mention a key point of your conversation].

I wanted to express my gratitude for the insightful exchange we had. Your perspectives on [Topic] were particularly intriguing and aligned well with our shared interests in [Common Interest]. I rarely come across someone who shares such a passion for [Specific Area], and I'm excited about the potential for collaboration.

In light of our discussion, I thought you might find the attached article on [Related Topic] interesting. It provides a fresh perspective on the challenges facing [Industry/Field]. I'd love to hear your thoughts on it and explore how we could apply some of these insights to our own work.

Please know that I value your time and understand how busy things can get. If you're available for a brief call next week, I'd be delighted to continue our conversation and explore potential opportunities for collaboration.

Looking forward to hearing from you and hopefully finding a suitable time for a call. Thank you again for your time and insights.

Best regards,

[Your Name]

[Your Title]

[Your Contact Information]

6. INTRODUCING COLLABORATIVE OPPORTUNITIES

In business, collaboration is often the catalyst for innovation and growth. Introducing Collaborative Opportunities via email is a strategic move that can open doors to partnerships, joint ventures, and mutually beneficial projects. By extending a hand of collaboration, you expand your network and demonstrate your willingness to work together toward shared objectives.

When you craft an email to introduce collaborative opportunities, you present a compelling partnership case. This could involve teaming up with like-minded professionals, complementary businesses, or industry experts to tackle challenges, leverage strengths, and create synergistic outcomes. Whether you're seeking to co-create products, share resources, or tap into new markets, this type of email can lay the foundation for powerful collaborations that yield lasting results.

A well-crafted email introducing collaborative opportunities should reflect genuine enthusiasm, showcase each party's value, and outline the potential benefits of working together. It's a delicate balance of showcasing your vision and understanding the needs and goals of your prospective partner.

| Template

Exploring Mutual Synergies for Future Success

Dear [Recipient's Name],

I hope this email finds you well. I have been following your impressive work in [Industry/Field], and I am truly inspired by the innovative approaches you bring to the table. Your dedication to [specific achievement or project] has not gone unnoticed, and I believe there might be exciting opportunities for us to collaborate.

At [Your Company Name], we share a vision of [common objective, e.g., driving sustainability, enhancing customer experiences], and I am confident that our combined expertise could lead to remarkable outcomes. I envision a partnership that leverages your strengths in [Recipient's Strength/Area of Expertise] and our proficiency in [Your Strength/Area of Expertise].

As we embark on this journey of potential collaboration, I'm excited about the possibilities we can unlock together. Our joint efforts could lead to [potential benefits, e.g., new market opportunities, increased customer engagement, and cost savings].

I would love the opportunity to discuss this further at your convenience. Would you be open to a brief call or meeting to explore how we might align our strategies and resources for mutual success? Your insights and perspective would be invaluable as we chart the path forward.

Please let me know a time that works best for you, and I'll accommodate your schedule. Thank you for considering this opportunity, and I look forward to the possibility of creating something exceptional together.

Warm regards,

[Your Name]

[Your Title]

[Your Contact Information]

7. COMPELLING PRODUCT/ SERVICE OFFERING

One of the most significant opportunities is the chance to present a compelling product or service offering. This is your moment to showcase your offerings' value, address your audience's pain points, and, ultimately, persuade them to take action.

An email with a compelling product or service offering goes beyond a mere description. It's a persuasive narrative that highlights not only the features and benefits but also taps into the emotions and aspirations of your recipients. When crafted effectively, this type of email has the power to captivate, resonate, and convert.

Your email should articulate how your product or service addresses a specific need or challenge your recipient faces. It's about connecting the dots between what you offer and how it can improve their lives, solve their problems, or enhance their business. This email should be concise yet impactful, convincing your audience that what you have is exactly what they need.

Template

Unlock [Specific Benefit] with [Your Product/Service]

Dear [Recipient's Name],

I hope this email finds you well. I wanted to introduce you to an exciting opportunity that I believe aligns perfectly with [Recipient's Company/Project] goals.

Are you tired of [Specific Pain Point]? Our [Your Product/Service Name] is designed to tackle this challenge head-on, offering you [Key Benefit #1], [Key Benefit #2], and [Key Benefit #3].

Here's what sets us apart:

- [Highlight a Unique Feature]: Our [Feature] guarantees [Result].
- [Share Testimonial or Success Story]: Just like [Client Name] experienced a [Positive Outcome], you too can [Desired Outcome].
- [Offer]: For a limited time, we're offering [Special Deal] to help you [Benefit].

I'd love to discuss how [Your Product/Service Name] can make a difference for [Recipient's Company/Project]. Let's schedule a call to explore the possibilities further.

Looking forward to the opportunity to connect.

Best regards,

[Your Name]

[Your Title]

[Your Contact Information]

8. NEGOTIATION AND PROPOSAL SUBMISSION

Negotiation and proposal submission is critical to forging successful partnerships, closing deals, and expanding your reach. These stages represent pivotal moments where your communication skills shine, enabling you to articulate your value proposition, address concerns, and ultimately secure agreements that drive your business forward.

A well-crafted proposal can be the key that unlocks doors to lucrative collaborations. It's not just about presenting facts and figures; it's about strategically positioning your offering to resonate with the needs and aspirations of your target audience. Your proposal should showcase your expertise, highlight the benefits your counterpart will receive, and address any potential concerns they might have.

Conversely, negotiation is the art of finding common ground, where both parties feel they're getting a fair deal. Successful negotiation involves active listening, empathy, and a clear understanding of what each party wants to achieve. It's about finding creative solutions for your goals and negotiation partners.

| Template

Elevating [Recipient Company Name] 's Success with [Your Offering]

Dear [Recipient's Name],

I hope this email finds you well. I've had the privilege of learning more about [Recipient Company Name] 's goals and vision, and I'm excited to share how our [Your Offering] can play a pivotal role in helping you achieve them.

Our team at [Your Company Name] is dedicated to delivering [Key Benefits and Features of Your Offering]. With a track record of [Brief Example or Testimonial], we are confident that our expertise aligns seamlessly with your objectives.

Here's how we envision partnering together:

- [Highlight Specific Value Points]
- [Address Possible Concerns or Objections]
- [Outline Project Timeline and Deliverables]

I'd love to schedule a call to discuss this proposal in detail and explore how we can customize our offering to meet your precise needs. Your success is our priority, and I'm committed to ensuring this collaboration yields exceptional results.

Please let me know your availability for a brief call next week. I look forward to the opportunity to connect and explore this partnership further.

Best regards,

[Your Name]

[Your Title]

[Your Contact Information]

9. HANDLING CUSTOMER INQUIRIES

In the dynamic business landscape, customer inquiries are like stepping stones that bridge potential customers with your products or services. Handling these inquiries effectively can distinguish between a successful transaction and a missed opportunity. Whether it's a simple question about your offerings or a more complex inquiry, your response sets the tone for the customer's perception of your professionalism, reliability, and commitment to their needs.

Navigating Customer Inquiries

Each customer inquiry is a chance to engage, educate, and establish trust. A well-crafted response addresses the customer's immediate concerns and showcases your dedication to their satisfaction. It's an opportunity to demonstrate that you value their interest and are readily available to provide the information they seek.

Handling customer inquiries requires a blend of efficiency, clarity, and empathy. You want to promptly provide accurate information while ensuring your communication reflects your brand's voice and values. Doing so positions yourself as a dependable partner in their decision-making process.

Template

Re: Your Inquiry About [Product/Service Name]

Dear [Customer's Name],

Thank you for contacting us with your inquiry about [product/service name]. We appreciate your interest and are thrilled to provide you with the information you seek.

I'm pleased to inform you that [briefly highlight key features or benefits of the product/service]. Our [product/service] is designed to [address a customer pain point or need], and we take pride in delivering [specific value proposition]. To address your query directly:

[Answer the customer's specific question clearly and concisely.]

Should you have any additional questions or require further clarification, please don't hesitate to ask. We're here to ensure you have all the information you need to make an informed decision.

If you're ready to move forward, you can find more details on our website [include website link] or by contacting our sales team at [sales team contact information].

Again, thank you for considering [your brand name] for your [product/service] needs. We look forward to the possibility of serving you and exceeding your expectations.

Best regards,

[Your Name]

[Your Title]

[Your Contact Information]

10. PERSUASIVE CALL TO ACTION

One of the most critical elements in email business writing is the call to action (CTA). A persuasive call to action serves as the bridge between your carefully crafted message and the desired response from your recipient. Whether it's encouraging a potential client to schedule a meeting, prompting a customer to make a purchase, or inspiring a partner to take the next collaborative step, a well-designed CTA can be the tipping point that transforms interest into action.

The art of persuasion lies in guiding your reader toward a specific outcome while maintaining their trust and respect. A persuasive CTA is strategic, compelling, and seamlessly integrated into your email's narrative. It offers a clear and enticing proposition, communicates value, and minimizes friction in the decision-making process.

To master the persuasive call to action, consider these key factors:

- **Clarity:** Your CTA should leave no room for ambiguity. Clearly communicate the desired action you want your recipient to take. Use specific language that leaves no doubt about what you're asking for.

- **Benefit:** Highlight the benefits of following through on the action. What will the recipient gain by taking the step you're proposing?

Address their needs, pain points, or aspirations to make your CTA more appealing.

- **Urgency:** Introduce an element of urgency to encourage immediate action. Limited-time offers, upcoming deadlines, or exclusive opportunities can create a sense of FOMO (fear of missing out) that spurs recipients into action.

- **Seamlessness:** Make it easy for the recipient to respond. If your CTA requires a click, ensure the link is prominently displayed and leads to a relevant landing page. If a reply is needed, clearly specify the necessary information.

- **Persuasive Language:** Use persuasive language that resonates with your audience. Address pain points, appeal to emotions, and emphasize the value of your proposed action.

- **Testing and Optimization:** Monitor the effectiveness of different CTAs and refine your approach based on data. A/B testing can help you identify which wording, design, or placement works best for your audience.

A persuasive call to action should not feel manipulative or forceful. Instead, it should align with your overall message and enhance the recipient's experience by guiding them toward a beneficial decision.

Template

Elevate Your [Recipient's Need] with [Your Solution]

Dear [Recipient's Name],

I hope this message finds you well. I've been thoroughly impressed by [recipient's project/achievements], and I believe there's a fantastic opportunity for us to collaborate.

Our [product/service] is designed to [solve recipient's specific problem or meet their need], and I'm confident it would make a significant impact on your [project/goal]. Clients who have adopted our solution have seen [specific results or benefits], and I'm excited to discuss how we can tailor it to your requirements.

I invite you to schedule a brief call with me to explore how [product/service] can revolutionize your [project/goal]. Let's take the first step toward [specific outcome] together.

Click here [insert link] to book a convenient time for our call. Should you have any questions, feel free to reach out. I'm here to provide any information you need.

Thank you for considering this opportunity, [Recipient's Name]. I'm looking forward to our conversation.

Best regards,

[Your Name]

[Your Contact Information]

11. LEVERAGING SOCIAL PROOF

Persuasion is an invaluable skill. It's about presenting your ideas, products, or services in a way that resonates with your audience, compelling them to take the desired action. One powerful technique in the art of persuasion is leveraging social proof.

The Power of Social Proof

Social proof is the psychological phenomenon where people tend to follow the actions of others, especially when they are uncertain about a decision. In email business writing, using social proof can significantly enhance your persuasiveness. You create a sense of trust and legitimacy when you demonstrate that others have benefited from your offerings or have taken similar actions.

Showcasing Success Stories

One of the most effective ways to leverage social proof is by showcasing success stories or testimonials. Highlight positive experiences from satisfied customers, clients, or partners who have achieved desirable outcomes through your product or service. These stories provide tangible evidence of the value you bring, helping to alleviate doubts and reinforce the credibility of your claims.

| Template

Transforming Businesses – Real Stories from Our Clients

Dear [Recipient's Name],

I hope this email finds you well. I wanted to share some inspiring success stories from clients who have partnered with us to transform their businesses. These stories speak to our solutions' impact on a wide range of industries.

[Client A's Story] "I was skeptical at first, but after implementing [Your Product/Service], our sales increased by 30% within just two months. The guidance and support provided by the [Your Company] team were instrumental in achieving these remarkable results."

[Client B's Story] "Working with [Your Company] revolutionized our approach to [Specific Challenge]. Our collaboration not only streamlined our processes but also saved us valuable time and resources. I can't thank the team enough for their expertise."

[Client C's Story] "As a [Industry] professional, I was seeking a partner who truly understood our unique challenges. [Your Company] not only understood but exceeded our expectations, delivering solutions that had an immediate positive impact."

These success stories are a testament to our dedication and expertise to every partnership. We are passionate about helping businesses like yours thrive and would love the opportunity to explore how we can work together.

If you'd like to learn more about our proven track record and how we can tailor our solutions to your needs, please don't hesitate to reach out. Let's discuss how we can help you achieve your business goals.

Warm regards,

[Your Name]

[Your Title]

[Your Contact Information]

12. NURTURING LEADS THROUGH EMAIL

Nurturing leads is akin to tending a garden. It requires patience, care, and a strategic approach. Just as gardener waters, fertilize, and watch over their plants, a savvy business professional nurtures leads through a series of well-crafted and thoughtful emails.

Lead nurturing involves building a relationship with potential clients over time. These leads might have shown initial interest in your product or service, but they're not quite ready to make a purchase. Your task is to guide them along the journey, providing value, addressing their concerns, and gently steering them toward a purchasing decision. This approach is not about pushing for an immediate sale but building trust and positioning your business as a reliable solution.

The Art of Lead-Nurturing Emails

Lead nurturing emails are your opportunity to showcase your expertise, understand your leads' needs, and foster genuine connections. These emails should be tailored to your leads' specific interests and pain points. Through strategic content, you can keep your brand top-of-mind, educate your leads, and gradually guide them toward becoming loyal customers.

A successful lead nurturing email sequence often starts with an introductory email that thanks the lead for their interest and sets expectations for future communication. Subsequent emails can deliver valuable insights, success stories, and case studies that demonstrate the benefits of your product or service. Interactive content, such as quizzes or webinars, can also engage leads and encourage them to interact with your brand.

Template

Unleash Your Business's Potential with [Your Product/Service]

Dear [Lead's Name],

I trust this email finds you well. I wanted to take a moment to express my gratitude for your interest in [Your Product/Service]. We believe that businesses like yours have incredible potential, and we're here to support you every step of the way.

In today's competitive landscape, staying ahead of the curve is crucial. That's why I'd like to share an exclusive resource with you: our latest eBook, "Unlocking Growth Strategies for Modern Businesses." This eBook delves into industry trends, innovative solutions, and actionable tips that can propel your business forward.

Download "Unlocking Growth Strategies for Modern Businesses" [Link to eBook] and discover:

- Proven strategies to increase your online presence
- Insights into customer engagement and retention
- Case studies showcasing real business success stories

We aim to provide you with valuable insights to drive your business's growth. Feel free to reach out with any questions or topics you'd like us to cover in future emails.

Thank you for being part of our community. We're excited to support you on your journey toward success.

Warm regards,

[Your Name]

[Your Title]

[Your Contact Information]

13. PROFESSIONAL CORRESPONDENCE

In the business world, formal and professional correspondence plays a pivotal role in maintaining relationships, conveying important information, and upholding the image of your organization. Whether you're communicating with clients, colleagues, superiors, or partners, how you present yourself and your ideas through email can significantly impact how you're perceived.

Professional correspondence goes beyond mere words; it reflects your attention to detail, respect for the recipient's time, and commitment to clear and concise communication. Well-crafted emails in formal situations exhibit your professionalism, ensuring that your message is taken seriously and your intent is clearly understood.

Whether you're communicating important updates, seeking guidance, or expressing appreciation, your emails should reflect the level of professionalism that's vital in today's business environment.

Template

Seeking Your Expertise and Guidance

Dear [Recipient's Name],

I hope this email finds you well. I am writing to seek your expert insights and guidance regarding [specific topic or challenge]. Your wealth of experience in [relevant field or area of expertise] makes you the ideal person to provide valuable insights.

I am currently facing [briefly describe the challenge or situation], and your perspective could illuminate potential solutions. I would greatly appreciate the opportunity to schedule a brief call or meeting at your convenience. Your input would be precious as I navigate this challenge.

Thank you for considering my request. I value your expertise and look forward to learning from your insights.

Best regards,

[Your Name]

[Your Title]

[Your Contact Information]

14. DELIVERING DIFFICULT NEWS

In business communication, not all messages are easy to convey. There come moments when you must address difficult news, whether it's informing a client of a delay in a project, communicating changes that might not be well-received, or delivering a message that could potentially lead to disappointment or concern. While such situations are challenging, they are crucial opportunities to demonstrate professionalism, empathy, and commitment to transparent communication.

The Role of Delivering Difficult News

Effectively delivering difficult news requires a delicate balance between honesty and empathy. As a business professional, you aim to provide clear and accurate information while also considering the recipient's feelings and potential reactions. By addressing challenging situations head-on and with sincerity, you maintain your integrity and uphold the trust that underpins successful business relationships.

This chapter will explore the art of delivering difficult news with compassion. You'll learn strategies for structuring your message, choosing the right tone, and offering solutions or alternatives whenever possible. Our goal is to equip you with the tools you need to navigate tough conversations in a way that maintains your reputation and fosters a sense of understanding between you and your recipient.

| Template

Update on Project Timeline

Dear [Client's Name],

I hope this message finds you well. I wanted to reach out to provide you with an update on the progress of our ongoing project.

While we have been working diligently to meet our initial timeline, unforeseen challenges have arisen that have impacted our ability to stay on schedule. Please know that we understand the importance of timely delivery and its impact on your goals.

We are committed to delivering a high-quality outcome. Given the current situation, we have adjusted our project plan to ensure the final result meets your expectations. We are taking the necessary steps to address these challenges and expedite the process without compromising the quality of our work.

I understand that this news may be disappointing, and I want to assure you that we are fully dedicated to resolving the situation and keeping you informed every step of the way. If you have any concerns or questions, please feel free to contact me directly.

Thank you for your understanding and ongoing support. We value your partnership and remain committed to delivering the best possible results.

Best regards,

[Your Name]

[Your Title]

[Your Contact Information]

15. JOB APPLICATION AND INTERVIEW FOLLOW-UP

E ffective communication must be considered when navigating the world of job applications and interviews. In an environment where competition is fierce and first impressions matter, the way you present yourself before, during, and after the interview can significantly influence the outcome. This chapter focuses on the delicate balance of professionalism, gratitude, and enthusiasm that defines successful job applications and interview follow-up emails.

Your journey toward landing that dream job doesn't end with submitting a polished resume or acing the interview. Instead, it extends into the realm of post-interview communication. Following up after an interview is not just a formality—it's an opportunity to reinforce your interest, showcase your appreciation for the opportunity, and leave a lasting impression on the hiring team.

Template

Re: [Position Title] Interview Follow-Up

Dear [Interviewer's Name],

I hope this email finds you well. I wanted to take a moment to express my sincere gratitude for the opportunity to interview for the [Position Title] role at [Company Name]. Discussing the [specific topics discussed] with you and the team was a pleasure.

After our conversation, I am even more excited about possibly joining [Company Name] and contributing to [relevant projects or initiatives]. Your insights about the company culture and the team's dedication to [key values or goals] truly resonated with me.

I am confident that my background in [mention specific skills or experiences relevant to the role] aligns well with the challenges and opportunities presented by the [Position Title] role. I am eager to bring my expertise to the team and contribute to [specific goals or projects].

If there are any additional details or information you require from my end, please don't hesitate to let me know. I look forward to working together and contributing to the continued success of [Company Name].

Thank you again for considering me for the [Position Title] position. I appreciate your time and consideration.

Warm regards,

[Your Full Name]

[Your Phone Number]

[Your Email Address]

CONCLUSION

Congratulations, you've reached the end of "**Effective Communication at Work: 15 Essential Email Templates for Business Communication.**" Throughout this journey, we've explored the art and science of effective email communication in business. From crafting impactful introductions to navigating formal situations and persuasive techniques, you've gained a valuable toolkit that can transform your professional communication.

As you reflect on your experience with this book, remember that email writing is not a one-size-fits-all endeavor. Each template and strategy you've encountered is a starting point, a foundation upon which you can build your own unique style and approach. Whether you're reaching out to potential clients, negotiating deals, nurturing relationships, or seeking career opportunities, your ability to communicate with clarity, professionalism, and persuasion will set you apart.

Continuing the Journey

While this book is a brief guide, improving your email business writing skills is ongoing. As you practice these templates and strategies, pay attention to what resonates with your audience, what elicits responses, and what fosters meaningful connections. Adapt, refine, and experiment with your approach to find what works best for your unique circumstances.

Remember that your emails are not just a means of transmitting information; they are opportunities to leave lasting impressions, forge connections, and drive action. Whether you're an entrepreneur, a corporate professional, or anyone looking to make an impact, your mastery of email business writing can be a powerful tool in your arsenal.

Thank you for embarking on this journey with us. We hope that "Effective Communication at Work: 15 Essential Email Templates for Business Communication" serves as a constant source of guidance and inspiration as you navigate the complex landscape of professional communication. Here's to your continued success in the world of business email writing!

www.ingramcontent.com/pod-product-compliance
Lightning Source LLC
Chambersburg PA
CBHW071521210326
41597CB00018B/2832